Conversational Prints

Decorative Fabrics of the 1950s

Joy Shih

Schiffer Publishing Ltd

4880 Lower Valley Road, Atglen, PA 19310

Acknowledgments

Thanks, Blair Loughrey, for your artistic skills, creativity, and for agreeing with me about what's cool. Oh yeah, assume the action stance, Scavenger Boy!

Sears Catalogs used with permission. Fall and Winter 1953, Philadelphia Edition 207, pp.755-761. Fall and Winter 1957, Atlanta Edition 215, pp.790-824. © Sears, Roebuck and Co.

Library of Congress Catalog Card Number: 97-80090
Copyright © 1997 by Schiffer Publishing

ISBN: 0-7643-0341-4
Printed in Hong Kong

Book Layout by: Blair Loughrey

Published by Schiffer Publishing Ltd.
4880 Lower Valley Road
Atglen, PA 19310
Phone: (610) 593-1777; Fax: (610) 593-2002
E-mail: Schifferbk@aol.com

Please write for a free catalog.
This book may be purchased from the publisher.
Include $3.95 for shipping.
Please try your bookstore first.

We are interested in hearing from authors
with book ideas on related subjects.

Contents

Dedication

To my pals, Bob Morris and Glenn Kinckner,

We've raised a lot of curtains together.
We think the 50s was pretty cool.
Music, art, the Jersey shore and Elvis...
Thanks for all the conversations after school.

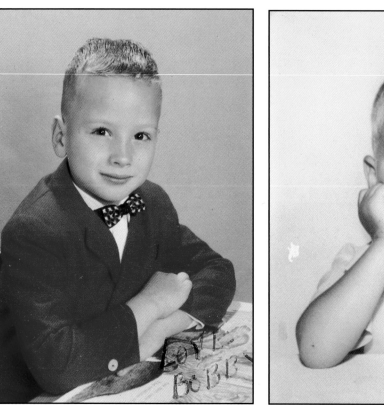

INTRODUCTION

Ah, the 1950s! We've all been there in one sense or another. Images from the era flood our collective memories. From grandmother's formica kitchen table to vintage '57 Chevy Bel Airs, from *I Love Lucy* to *Happy Days*, from diners to drive-ins, we continue to perpetuate the magic of that glorious decade today. Perhaps the most common experience that many Americans share was that fiesta cafe curtain in the kitchen window, the Hawaiian scene drapes in the living room, the nautical print chair in the den, or the Cowboys and Indians sheets on Johnny's bed.

Welcome back to the land of the 1950s conversational print. What are conversational prints, you ask? Other than your typical florals, polka dots, stripes, and plaids, essentially all other types of designs are called "novelty" or "conversational." These decorative fabrics, especially if the designs are small, are sometimes used as fabrics to wear. The majority however, due to the large designs and the interesting subjects, are primarily used for decorative purposes. The conversational print was a favorite for home decorating during the 1950s, appearing in not only window coverings but on sheets, tablecloths, aprons, and slipcovers.

It is true that how we decorate our homes is reflective of the culture in which we live. Consider the 1950s conversational print. It is postwar America. There's a baby boom going on strong. Television and movies catered to the growing juvenile market with westerns and circus theme shows. The nation at peace meant people started thinking about leisurely pastimes such as sports, sailing and other recreational activities. Air travel suddenly made the world a smaller place. Returning servicemen brought back stories of exotic destinations and grand European cities. Mexico was affordable, close enough to drive to, yet "foreign" enough to be considered an "exotic" place. The automobile became a

The ultimate in a conversational print. Black, orange, green, and blue on white. Cotton chintz.

Revolutionary war theme, engraved-look print. Cherry red on bone white. Cotton chintz.

staple for families who ventured out from the cities into new subdivisions and communities, creating a new culture known as Suburbia. Americana themes provided warm patriotic touches. Homey kitchen prints gave a feeling of apple pie family values. All these images, real or imagined, were transported onto fabrics decorating the inner sanctum of each family - the American home.

The designs on the following pages are taken from numerous American textile manufacturers' pattern books of the 1950s. Most of the fabrics are cotton or a cotton blend, which were durable and washable. Finishes on the fabrics gave the textile shape or "drapeability" as well as lend resistance to dirt. On many of the fabric swatches, the brown stains are remnants of the glue used to attach the samples to the pages. Although some of the swatches are small and do not show repeats, the designs presented were the ones the manufacturer deemed most saleable. Some of the fabric designs are shown in different colorways or color combinations to provide the reader an appreciation of decorative colors popular during the era, as well as the creativity of the designer.

Look at these wonderful designs as a tour of the 1950s home. I remember remodeling the kitchen in my postwar-built home. After tearing out the old appliances and cabinets, we were surprised to find 1950s-era wallpaper decorated with Grecian urns and boomerang shapes. I imagined the house as it might have looked during that time. These fabrics might do the same for you. For those of us who were around during the 50s, the designs will certainly bring back long-ago "conversations" around the kitchen table or in the family living room.

Happy memories, America.

AMERICANA WEST

Western Pioneers

Pioneer-theme scenes on pale yellow. Polished cotton.

Variation of the pioneer scenes print on beige.

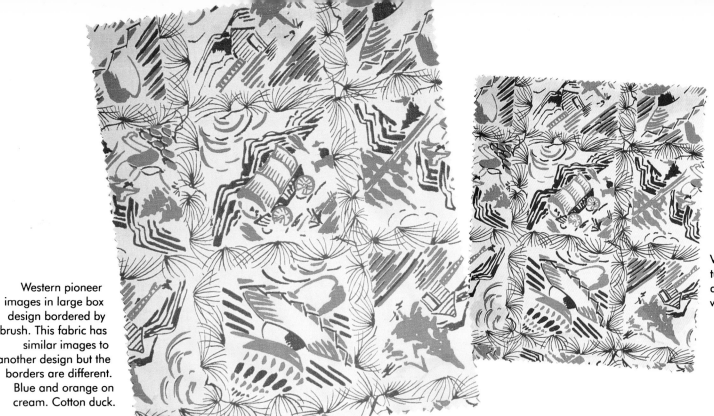

Western pioneer images in large box design bordered by brush. This fabric has similar images to another design but the borders are different. Blue and orange on cream. Cotton duck.

Variation in turquoise and dark brown on white.

Western pioneer theme design in a two-directional, boxed-pattern bordered with a chevron pattern. Blue and orange-brown on beige. Cotton and linen.

Two-directional, boxed-pattern with chevron designs on the borders. Pioneer-theme print. Green, red, and blue on yellow. Linen-look rayon.

California images including the old flag, and featuring the gold rush. Light blue and pink on taupe. Cotton chintz.

Colorful scenes depicting gold mining in the 1800s. Red, brown, blue, black, and yellow on white. Polished cotton.

Variation of the design on blue, green, yellow, and black on white background.

Another variation in a bolder color combination of red, green, yellow, and black on white.

Southwestern

Geometric design featuring southwestern vegetation. Gold and black on off-white. Polished cotton.

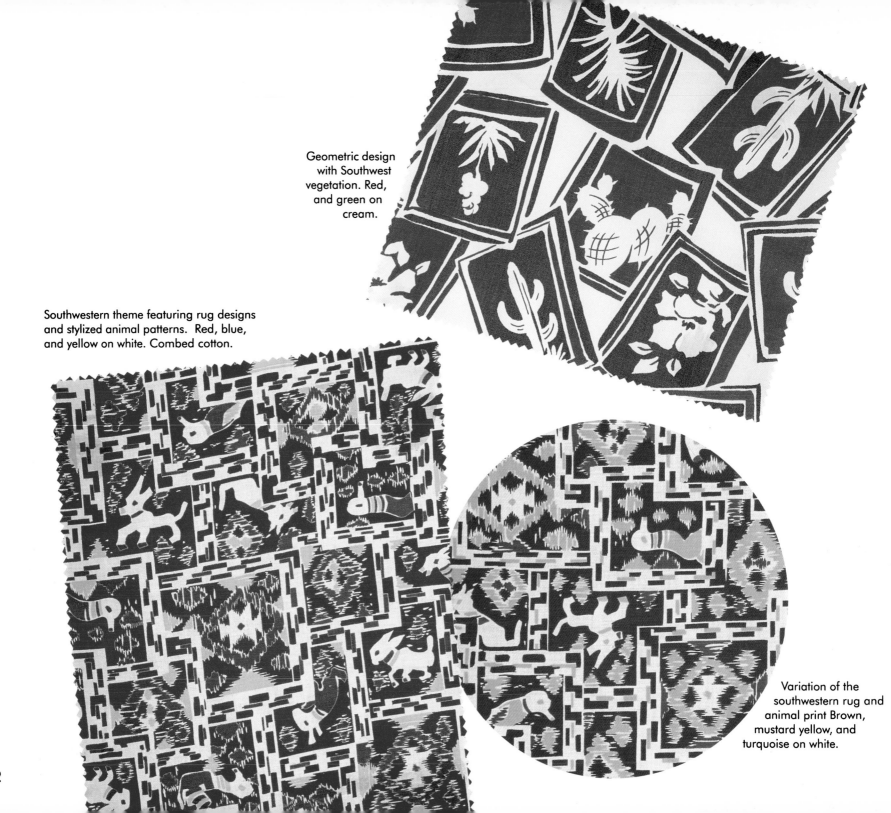

Geometric design with Southwest vegetation. Red, and green on cream.

Southwestern theme featuring rug designs and stylized animal patterns. Red, blue, and yellow on white. Combed cotton.

Variation of the southwestern rug and animal print Brown, mustard yellow, and turquoise on white.

The well-equipped cowboy needed these items to be in business. The large images are connected by ropes in a circular looping pattern. Mustard yellow, brown, and green on sky blue ground. Cotton chintz.

Cowboys and Indians

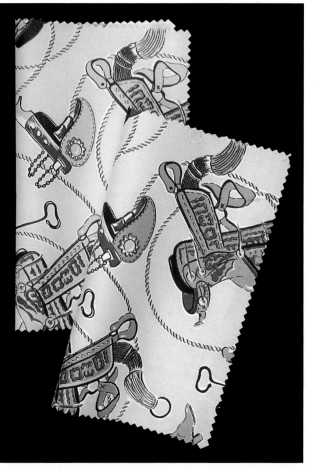

Two variations of the same fabric on pale yellow and sand backgrounds.

American West themes were popular during the 1950s. This design features the typical scenes of rodeo riders, western homesteads, Native American teepees, covered wagons, and cacti. Red, green, and gold on light blue ground. Cotton/rayon twill.

The same fabric in a different color variation. Multicolors on cream.

Western rodeo scenes on fence posts that form a modified plaid pattern. Red and browns on pale yellow. Cotton seersucker.

Two color variations of the same fabric on light blue and peach.

Two color variations on cream and yellow grounds.

Cowboy theme print. Red and yellow on pale blue. Combed cotton.

Branding day on the ranch. The rodeo clown in the polka dot outfit is barely visible on this swatch. Red, white, and taupe on blue ground. Cotton/rayon Poplin.

Two variations of the fabric on yellow and beige.

15

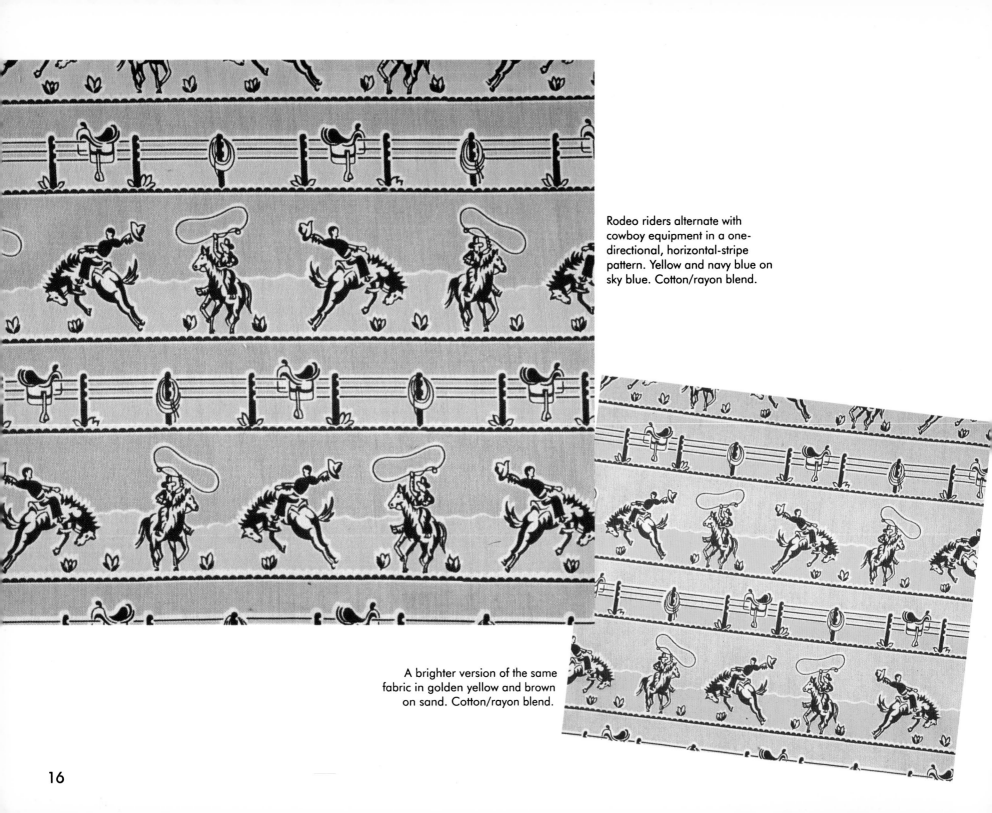

Rodeo riders alternate with cowboy equipment in a one-directional, horizontal-stripe pattern. Yellow and navy blue on sky blue. Cotton/rayon blend.

A brighter version of the same fabric in golden yellow and brown on sand. Cotton/rayon blend.

Cowboys roping bulls. Red and medium blue on sky blue. Polished cotton.

Two variations on sand
and yellow grounds.

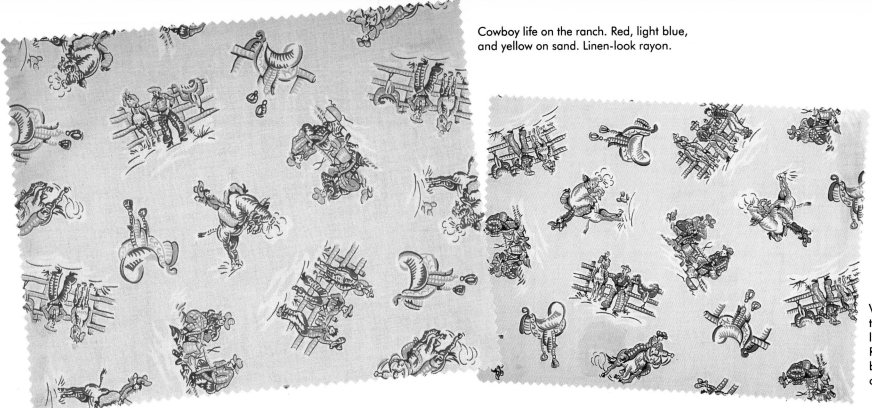

Cowboy life on the ranch. Red, light blue, and yellow on sand. Linen-look rayon.

Variation of the cowboy life fabric. Red, light blue, green on yellow.

Roping and branding images with scattered branding patterns. Red and light blue on sand. Cotton chintz.

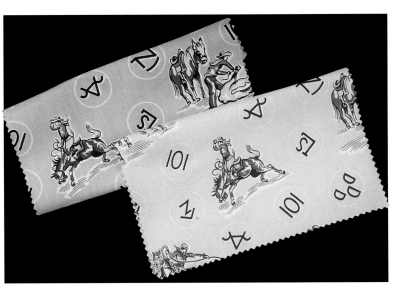

Variations of the same design on blue and yellow.

Two variations of the same design.

Silhouettes of rodeo riders are scattered on a cross-hatched basketweave pattern.
Dark green silhouettes on light green, orange, yellow and white. Linen-look rayon.

Large images of roping cowboys. Red, beige, and green on yellow. Linen-look rayon.

Branding designs. Chocolate brown on off-white. Cotton percale.

Two variations in colors on beige and light blue.

Two variations shown on taupe and pale yellow.

Square-dancing cowboys and "calls." Primary colors on light blue. Polished cotton.

Stagecoach border print on gingham background. Wagon wheels form a smaller border. Orange, red, and yellow on blue and white. Cotton chintz.

Cowboys and Indians battle in this print. It's hard to imagine that such violent images were used in popular western prints primarily geared to children. Red, blue, and green on yellow. Cotton/rayon blend.

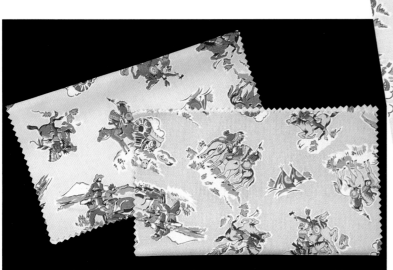

Color variations on light blue and tan.

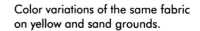

Color variations of the same fabric on yellow and sand grounds.

This one-directional border print depicts Indians attacking a stage coach. Stereotypical images of violent Native Americans were common in the 1950s. Red, green, and dark blue on tan. Linen-look rayon.

Native American-inspired print with feather motif. Green, golden yellow, brown, and white on beige. Cotton chintz.

Two variations of the Native American-inspired feather print on yellow and blue grounds.

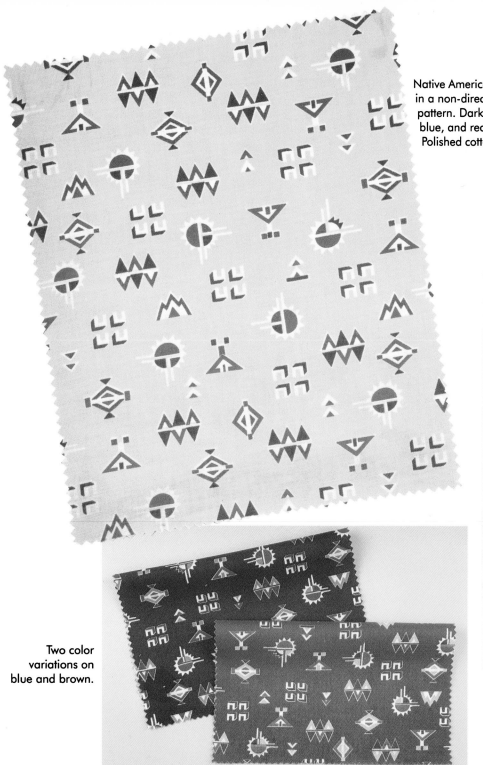

Native American symbols in a non-directional set pattern. Dark brown, blue, and red on yellow. Polished cotton.

Two color variations on blue and brown.

Native American motifs. Multi-colors on cream. Cotton/rayon blend.

25

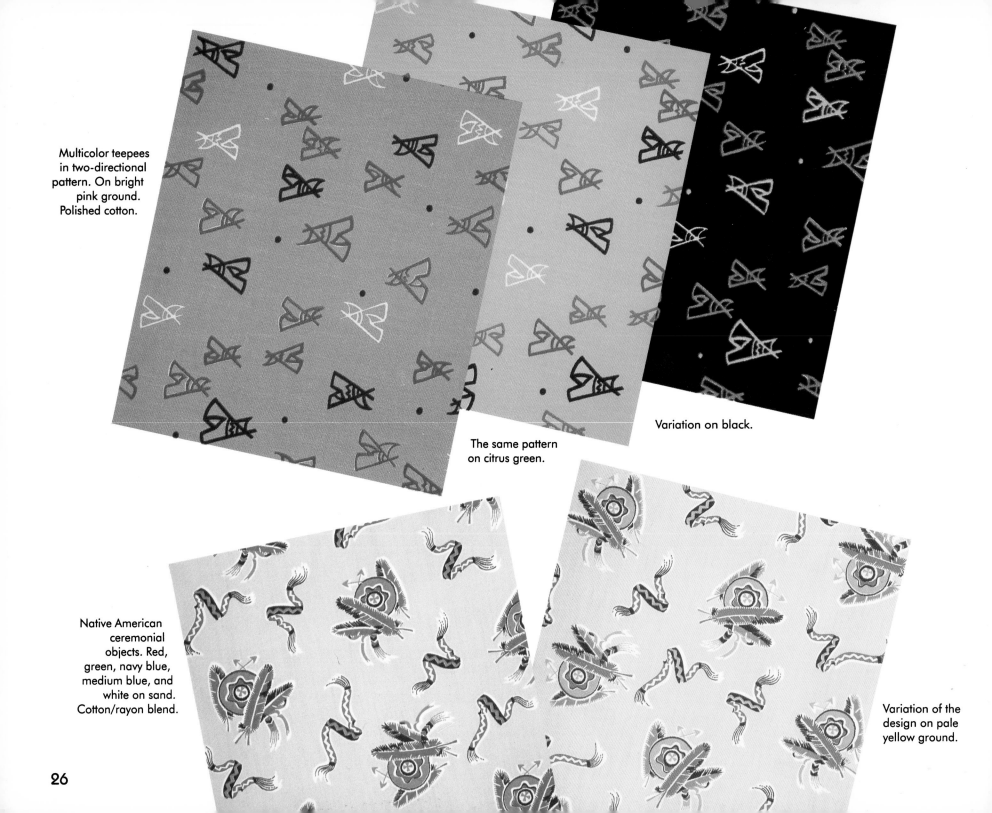

Multicolor teepees in two-directional pattern. On bright pink ground. Polished cotton.

The same pattern on citrus green.

Variation on black.

Native American ceremonial objects. Red, green, navy blue, medium blue, and white on sand. Cotton/rayon blend.

Variation of the design on pale yellow ground.

26

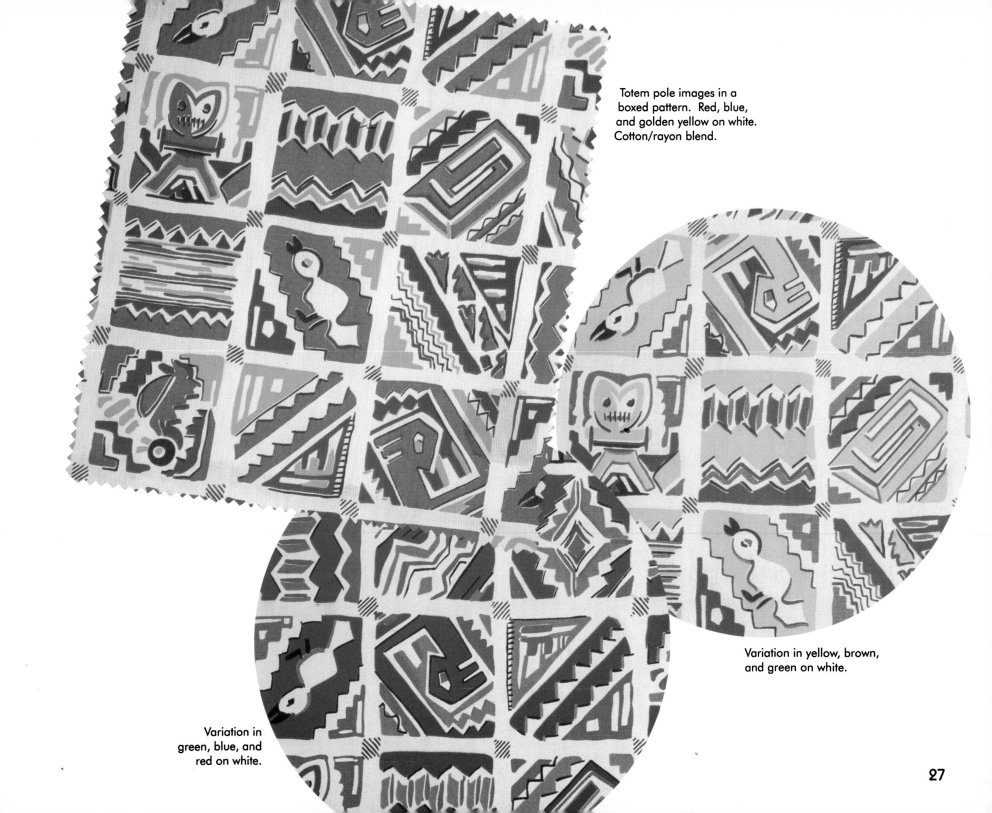

Totem pole images in a
boxed pattern. Red, blue,
and golden yellow on white.
Cotton/rayon blend.

Variation in yellow, brown,
and green on white.

Variation in
green, blue, and
red on white.

Variation of the same pattern in red, yellow, green, and black on sky blue.

Two-directional stripe pattern with Native American motifs. The teepee and drum border indicates that this is a vertical stripe pattern. Red, blue, green, and black on sand. Cotton/rayon blend.

Variation of the same pattern in blue, red, green, and brown on pale yellow.

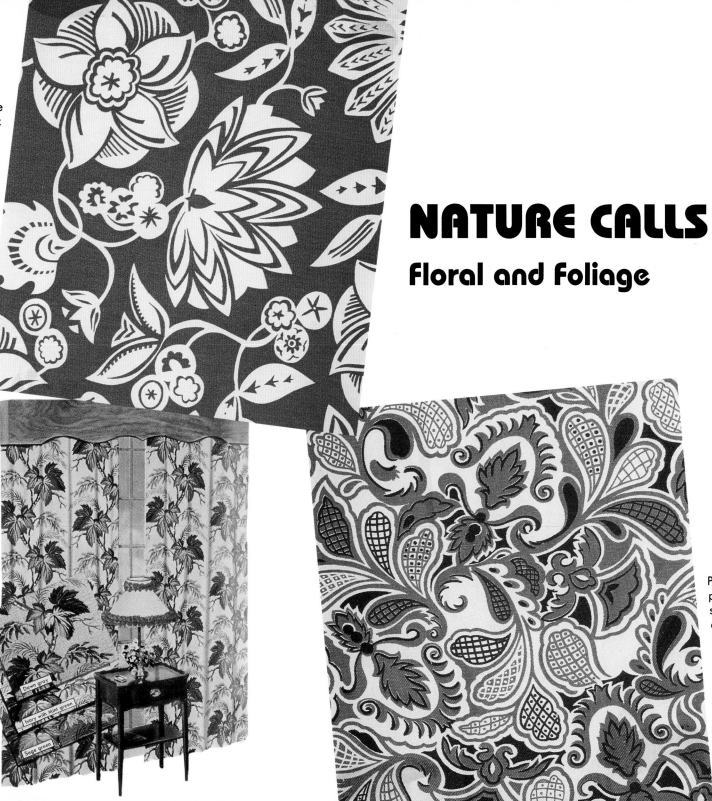

Stylized floral with the look of an Asian block print. Non-directional, monotone design. White on cocoa brown. Rayon.

NATURE CALLS

Floral and Foliage

Paisley floral pattern. Various shades of blue on cream. Cotton twill.

Down gray

Ivory with Mint green

Sage green

Stylized leaf pattern with paisley-like effect. Red, brown, and green on cream. Cotton chintz.

Two variations of the same pattern shown sand and light blue grounds.

Variation in brown, taupe, and orange on dark navy blue.

A lighter variation on pale yellow makes it look like a different design.

The large, broad leaves in this tropical jungle design are filled with a picotage striated design. Multicolor leaves on burgundy ground. Cotton/ rayon twill.

Monotone print of tropical foliage, leaves and bamboo. Black on light yellow ground. Cotton.

Variation of tropical foliage, leaves and bamboo print. Red on light yellow ground.

The flowing leaves of this foliage design lends movement to a simple monochromatic print. Green on cream. Polished cotton.

Two variations of the flowing leaves foliage print. Shown in blue and burgundy.

31

Flowering branches and fern print with a tropical feel. Terra cotta, white, and black on gray. Polished cotton.

Variation of the flowering branches and fern print. Red, white, and black on slate blue.

32

Palm trees superimposed with a color-on-color non-directional pattern. If this design was done a decade later, one might think this to be a marijuana plant. Rust, yellow, and green on white. Cotton chintz.

Two variations of the same fabric.

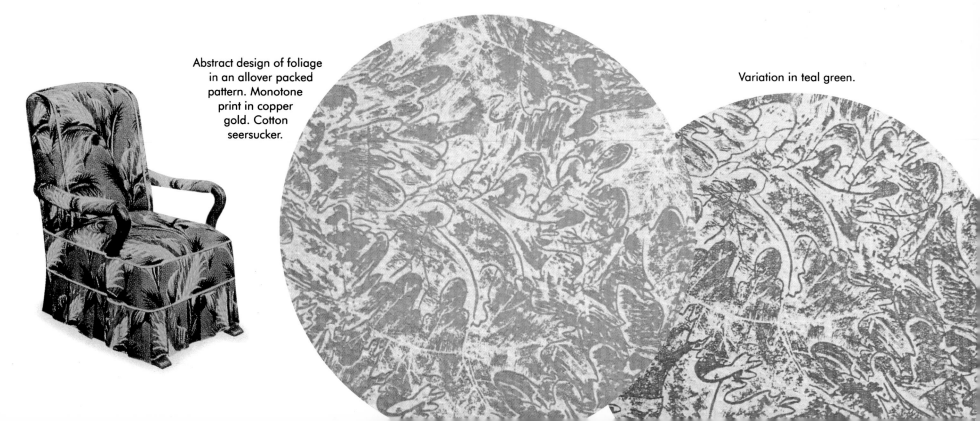

Abstract design of foliage in an allover packed pattern. Monotone print in copper gold. Cotton seersucker.

Variation in teal green.

Fish, Insects, Birds

Colorful ocean motif design with fish and starfish in a two-directional print. Cotton seersucker.

Goldfish design in a non-directional print. Red, blue, gray, and yellow on white ground. Cotton/rayon blend.

Two variations of the goldfish design. Brown, taupe, blue, and yellow on white, and Reddish brown, gray, deep aqua, and yellow on white.

Closeup of the underwater scene on two different fabrics. Combed cotton on top, cotton/rayon twill below.

Underwater fish scene in a bright monotone, allover non-directional print. Royal blue on light blue. Cotton/rayon twill.

Variation of the underwater scene print. Chocolate brown on cream.

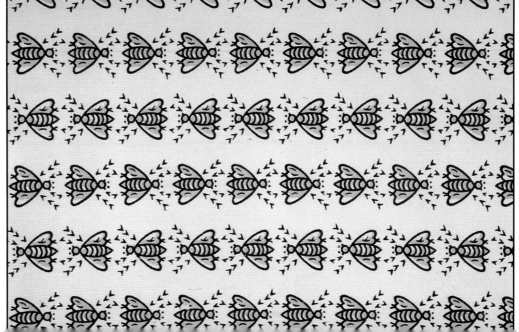

Buzzing bees in a two-directional, set pattern. Yellow and black on white. Pinwale cotton corduroy.

Fun print featuring penguins on ice floes. Red and teal green on sand. Cotton/rayon twill.

Two variations of the penguin print in royal blue and red on light blue, and brown and light blue on sand.

Fancy bird cages in two-directional pattern. Cream ground. Cotton chintz.

Big pattern of foliage, fruit, and birds in an Oriental-look design. Multicolors on white ground. Brushed cotton.

Color variation of the same pattern.

Color variation of the same pattern.

Dawn gray C

Spice brown

WATER, WATER, EVERYWHERE

Ocean Life

Large images of frolicking whales in a bold, non-directional print. Brown and blue on white. Cotton chintz.

Variations of the whale print. Red and gray on white, and Black and yellow on white.

Shell motif in a stylized design. Blue, yellow, green, and brown on cream ground. Cotton/rayon blend.

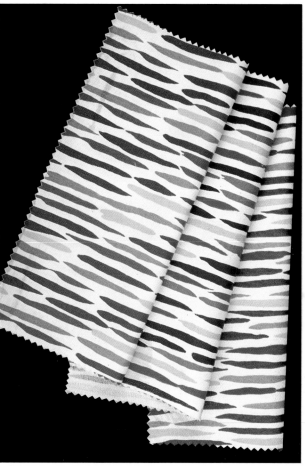

Modified stripes give this design a rippling water surface effect. Shown in three variations on white ground. Combed cotton.

39

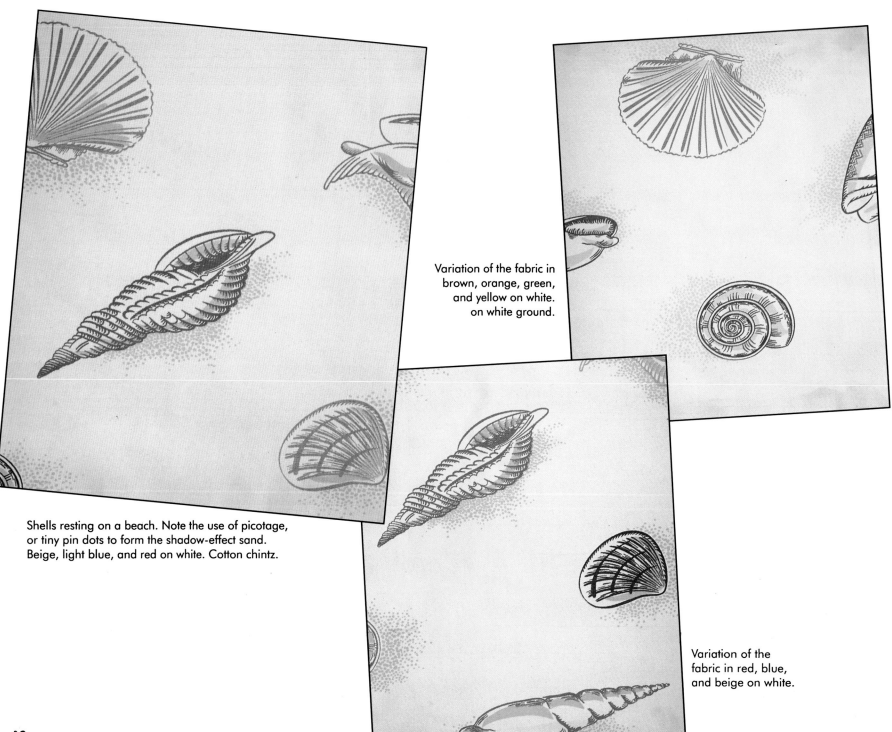

Variation of the fabric in
brown, orange, green,
and yellow on white.
on white ground.

Shells resting on a beach. Note the use of picotage,
or tiny pin dots to form the shadow-effect sand.
Beige, light blue, and red on white. Cotton chintz.

Variation of the
fabric in red, blue,
and beige on white.

Border design featuring children playing on a beach. Reds and blues on pale yellow ground. Cotton-rayon blend.

Fun on the Beach

Variation of the border design. Red and aqua on pale yellow ground.

Variation of the beach sports theme print. Red, blue, and grey on white.

Variation of the beach sports theme print. Red, brown, and olive green on white.

Beach sports theme with beach balls and diving scenes. Brown and green designs, yellow strokes on off-white ground. Although the beach designs appear in a non-directional pattern, this fabric is probably a two-directional print with the yellow wave-like strokes running in a horizontal fashion. Polished cotton.

Sailing vessels. Rust brown on cream. Polished cotton.

Nautical Motifs

Variation of sailing vessels. Kelly green on very pale aqua.

Bright print of sail boats and sweeping cypress trees. Red, blue, and taupe on white. Cotton/rayon blend.

43

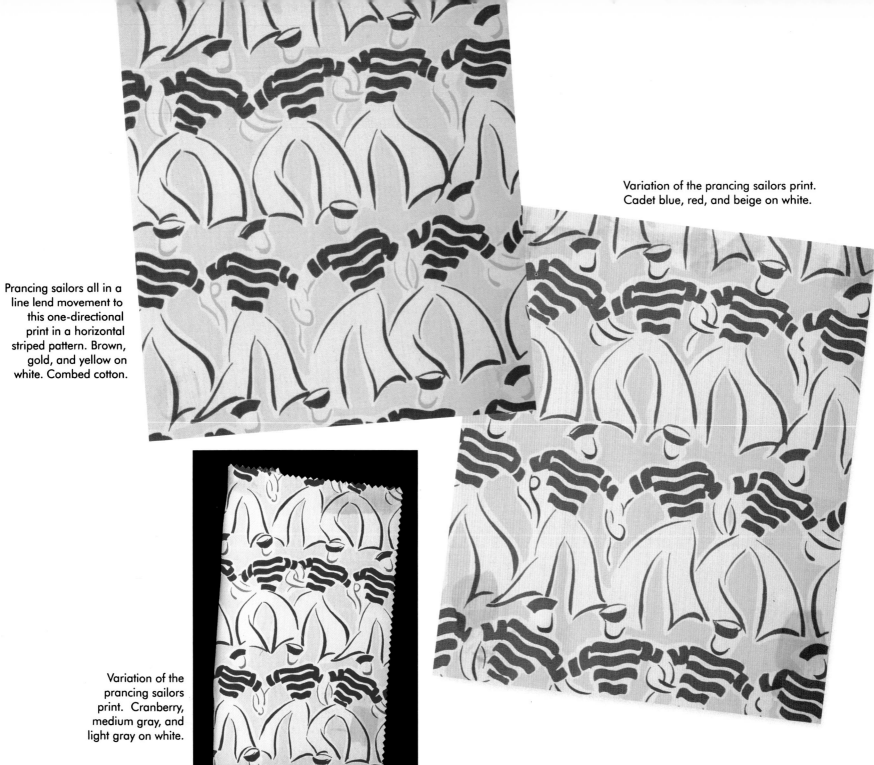

Variation of the prancing sailors print. Cadet blue, red, and beige on white.

Prancing sailors all in a line lend movement to this one-directional print in a horizontal striped pattern. Brown, gold, and yellow on white. Combed cotton.

Variation of the prancing sailors print. Cranberry, medium gray, and light gray on white.

44

A nautical theme print with a variety of sailing and ocean motifs. Red, blue, and yellow on cream. Polished cotton.

Variation of the nautical theme print. Red, brown, golden yellow, and green on cream.

Bright print featuring sailboats framed by ropes and lifesaver rings. Yellow and white on bright red. Cotton/rayon blend.

Images inspired by the novel *Moby Dick*. Blue, brown and black on very pale yellow. Cotton chintz.

Two variations on yellow and blue grounds.

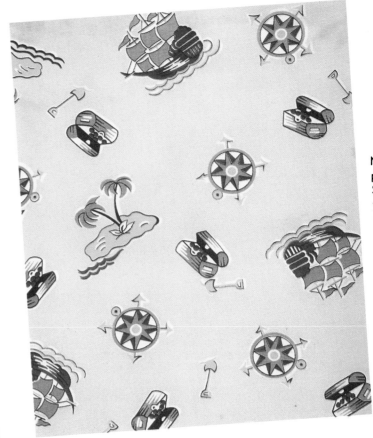

Nautical images in a pirate theme print. Slate blue, red, and yellow on light yellow ground. Cotton twill.

Lighthouses, seagulls, and anchors. Red, blue, and white on pale yellow. Cotton chintz.

Variation of the fabric in red, brown, white on pale yellow.

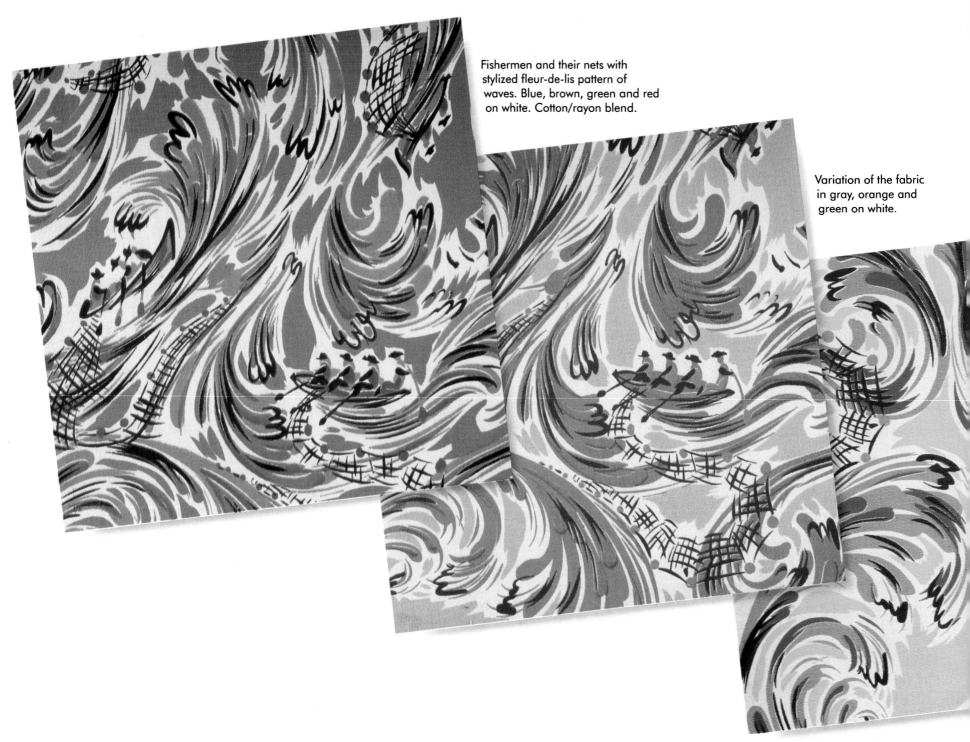

Fishermen and their nets with stylized fleur-de-lis pattern of waves. Blue, brown, green and red on white. Cotton/rayon blend.

Variation of the fabric in gray, orange and green on white.

48

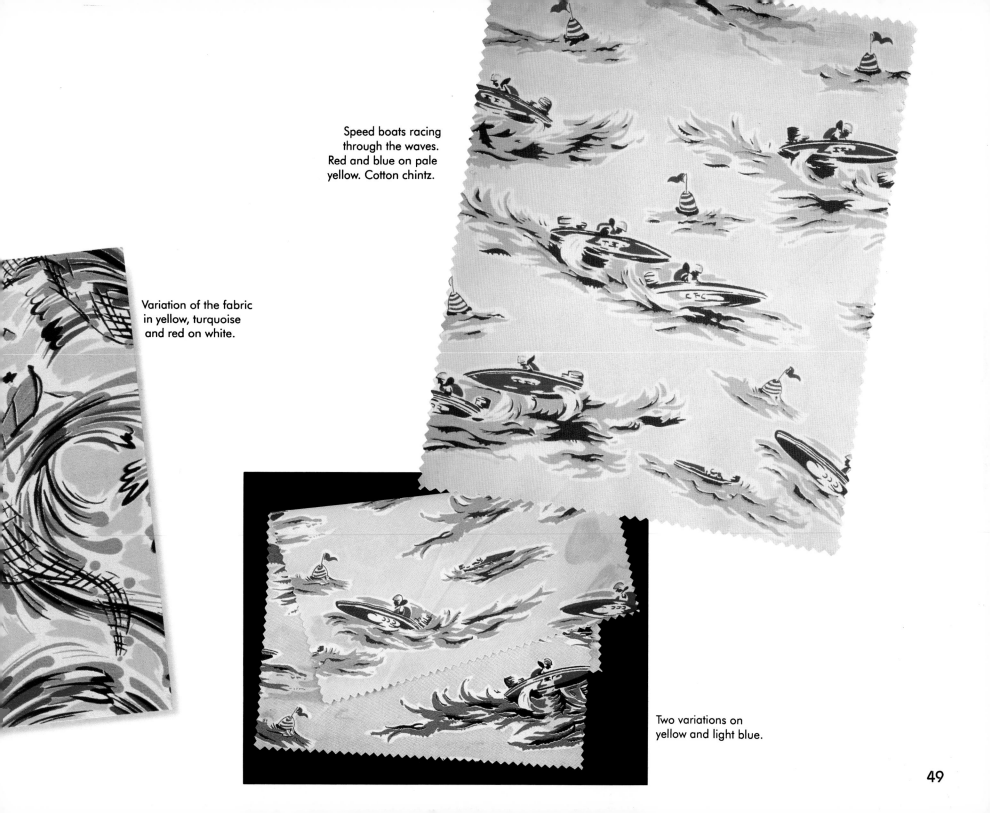

Speed boats racing
through the waves.
Red and blue on pale
yellow. Cotton chintz.

Variation of the fabric
in yellow, turquoise
and red on white.

Two variations on
yellow and light blue.

49

EXOTIC DESTINATIONS

Tropical Scenes

Tropical river scene in a
two-directional print.
Navy, red, and gray on
white ground. Cotton-
backed linen.

Variation of the
tropical river
scene. Turquoise
brown, and gra
on pale yellow.

This water-skiing design is placed in the tropical section due to the mountain background scenes and the brown-skinned figures. Red, gray, and blue on white ground. Polished cotton.

Variation of the tropical water-skiing print. Predominantly gray.

51

Tiki boats and large flying birds. Brown, yellow, and green on pale yellow ground. Combed cotton/polyester blend.

Variation of the tiki boats and flying birds print. Red, green, yellow, and white on taupe.

Variation of the tiki boats and flying birds print. Burgundy, medium blue, yellow, and white on sky blue.

52

Polynesian village scene two-directional print with large palm trees and boats with tapa sails. Red, golden yellow, and navy blue on pale yellow ground. Cotton/rayon blend.

Variation of the Polynesian village scene print. Burgundy, blue, and yellow on gray ground. Cotton/rayon blend.

Polynesian village scene print. Close-up of same design, in the same colors, but in a different fabric. Linen-look rayon.

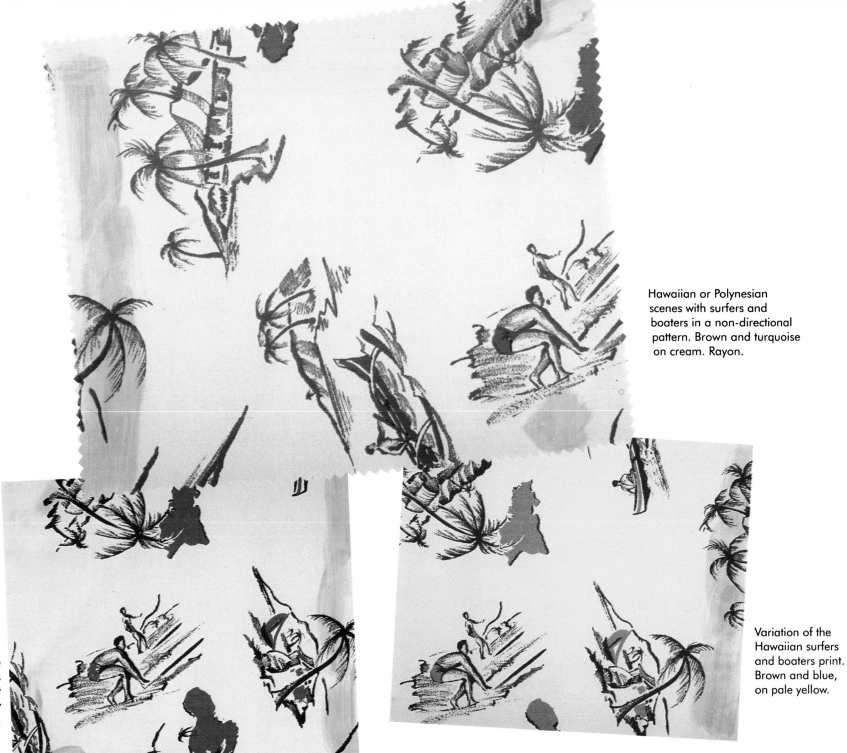

Hawaiian or Polynesian scenes with surfers and boaters in a non-directional pattern. Brown and turquoise on cream. Rayon.

Variation of the Hawaiian surfers and boaters print Blue and cranberry on white.

Variation of the Hawaiian surfers and boaters print. Brown and blue, on pale yellow.

54

Straw huts provide a setting for the large foliage in this tropical design. Green, red, and slate blue on pale gray ground. Polished cotton.

Variation of the fabric in Red, blue, green, and yellow on cream.

Islands of palm trees on shimmering water in a two-directional print. Dark brown on pale aqua. Cotton/rayon blend.

Variation of the palm trees print. Navy blue on yellow.

The ultimate in deep sea fishing.
The large images are spaced
between blue wave-effect strokes.
Coral red, medium brown, and
blue on white. Cotton rayon.

Variation of the
deep sea fishing
print. Green,
brown, and
yellow on white.

Variation of the deep sea fishing print. Yellow, brown, and greenish gray on white.

Deep sea fishing, coordinating print featuring smaller images. Green, brown, and yellow on white. Cotton rayon.

The two coordinating prints are shown together for a better perspective on the size of the images in the fabric design.

Scattered images of shells, boats, and tropical palm trees. Red, green, and yellow on sand. Cotton twill.

Variation of the design in red, yellow, and blue on pale yellow ground.

Hawaiian scenes framed by bamboo. Red, blue, and gold on white. Cotton/linen blend.

Two variations of the same pattern on yellow and red backgrounds.

Tropical village and cove scenes. Red, green, and dark gray on gray. Cotton chintz.

Variation of design in green, blue, and red on cream background

Florida cities and scenes. Coral and dark blue on white. Linen.

Two variations on light blue and pale pink. The pair of sunglasses give this a touristy feel.

59

Left:
Tropical village scene.
Turquoise, purple, and black
on white. Cotton chintz.

Above:
Variation in red, yellow,
and black on white.

60

Bottom of a border print featuring Caribbean posters on a faux woven background. Cotton chintz.

Smaller images from the same border print.

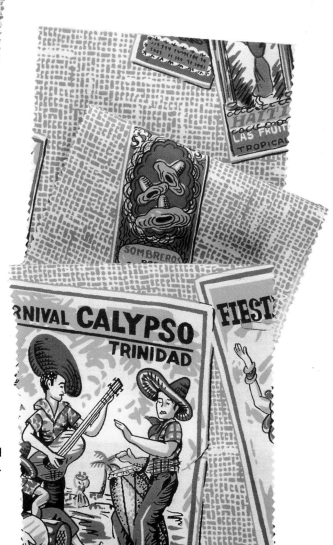

Both smaller and larger border images.

Mexican Images

Border print with Mexican village theme. Unfortunately, a larger swatch of this fabric was not available to determine the rest of the design. This swatch was probably determined by the manufacturer to be the most interesting portion of the design. Turquoise, yellow, and red. Cotton duck.

Three variations of a border print with Mayan-inspired designs. The Mayan civilization existed in Central America in parts of Guatemala, Honduras and the coastal regions of Mexico. The fascination with Mexico as an exotic locale during the 1950s probably inspired this print. Cotton chintz.

Mexican cowboys parading through town. Blue and beige on sky blue ground. Linen-look rayon.

Mexican images framed in octagonal block patterns. Kelly green, red, and golden yellow on off-white. Polished cotton.

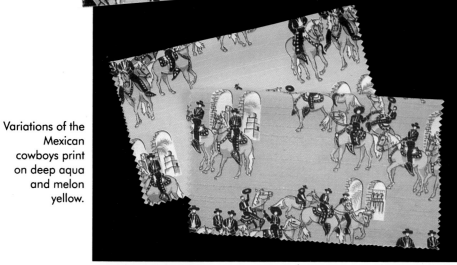

Variations of the Mexican cowboys print on deep aqua and melon yellow.

Two variations of the same print.

Sombreros and cactus float in a scattered small print. Red, golden yellow, blue, and white on pale yellow ground. Cotton/rayon blend.

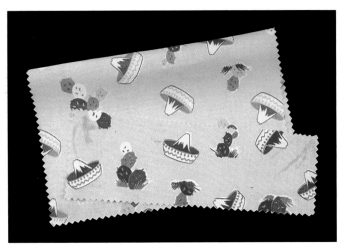

Two variations on sky blue and sand.

Two color variations of the same design.

Mexican images in a swirling pattern. Pink and green on white. Cotton/polyester blend.

Mexican themes framed with a rope border. Red, blue, and green on sand. Linen-look rayon.

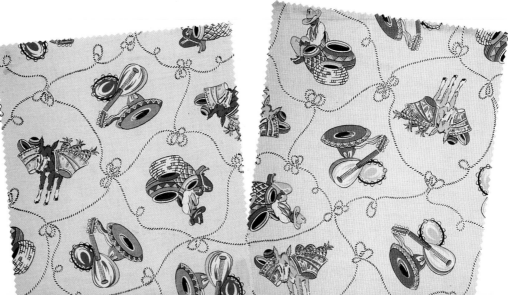

Variation in red and green on pale yellow.

Variation in yellow, brown, and green on cream.

65

Around the World

Architectural elements from around the world, overlaid with a thin beehive grid. Blue and green on white. Cotton/rayon blend.

Variation in green and pink.

Closeup of the fabric design in orange yellow, and gray.

Closeup of the fabric design shown in blues and purples.

67

Primitive hunting images, in a South American-inspired print. Navy blue on light blue. Cotton/rayon blend.

Variation in taupe, cadet blue, black and white.

French newspaper theme with city scenes. Orange, gray, black and white. Cotton.

Variations in purple, olive green, black and white.

European city scenes with cartoon images. Olive and teal on white. Cotton/polyester blend.

Oversize border design of a French city scene, shown near bottom border. Yellow, brown, and green on white. Cotton/polyester blend.

Scene just above the border design.

Closeup of the same design in aqua, green, and blue on white.

Closeup of the same design in bright pink, red, and green on white.

Images of Holland. Salmon, brown, blue, and bright green on white. Cotton/polyester blend.

Dutch figures and assorted images on dotted ground. Blue and white on brown. Polyester crepe.

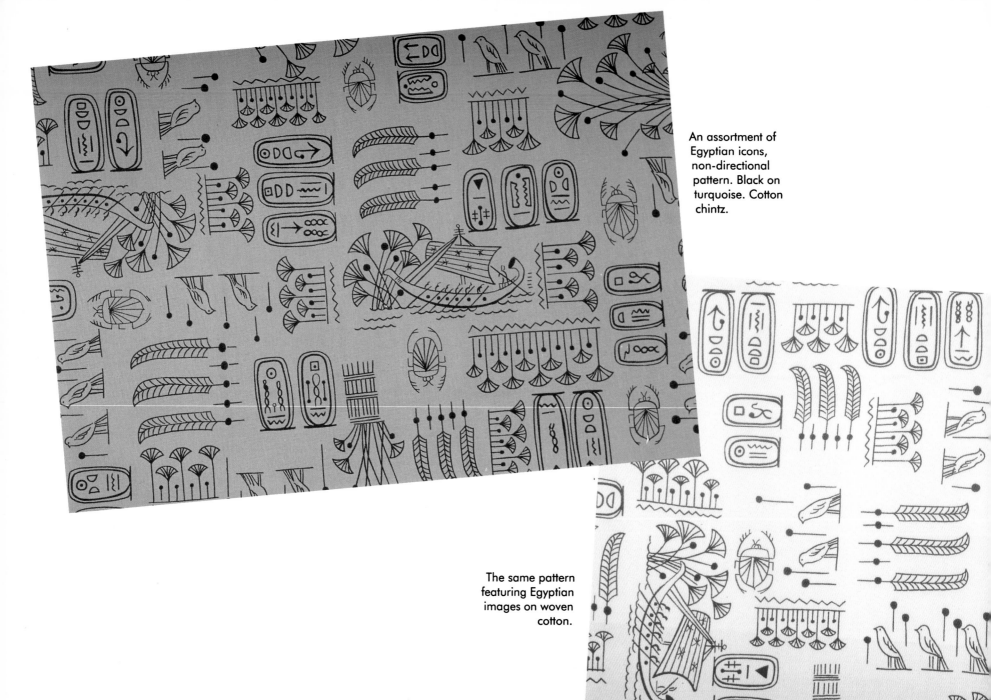

An assortment of Egyptian icons, non-directional pattern. Black on turquoise. Cotton chintz.

The same pattern featuring Egyptian images on woven cotton.

72

Closeup of the same pattern on bright red.

Oriental motifs in a two-directional orderly pattern.
Shown in three color variations. Cotton/polyester blend.

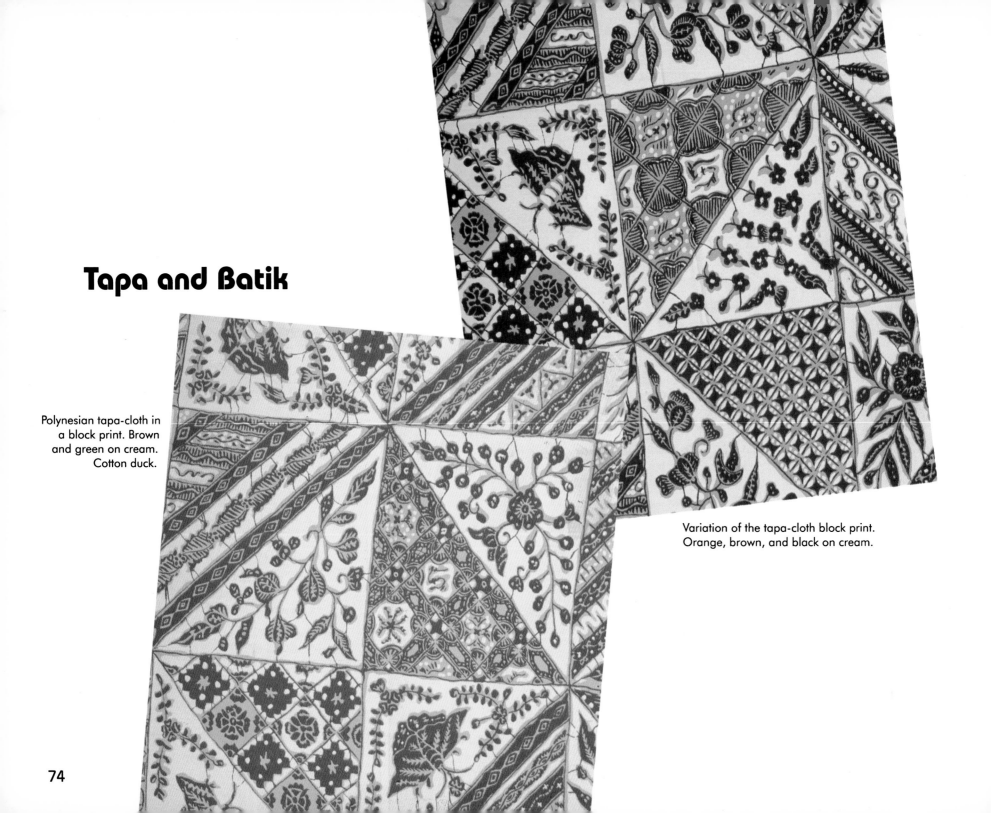

Tapa and Batik

Polynesian tapa-cloth in
a block print. Brown
and green on cream.
Cotton duck.

Variation of the tapa-cloth block print.
Orange, brown, and black on cream.

74

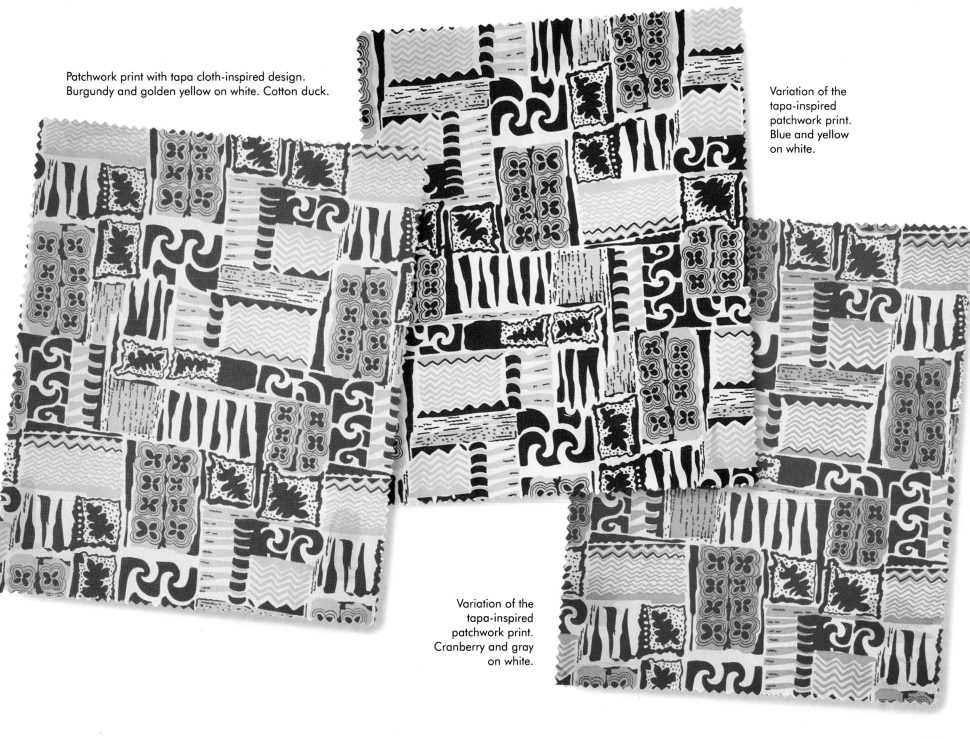

Patchwork print with tapa cloth-inspired design. Burgundy and golden yellow on white. Cotton duck.

Variation of the tapa-inspired patchwork print. Blue and yellow on white.

Variation of the tapa-inspired patchwork print. Cranberry and gray on white.

75

Tapa-inspired print in a
stylized paisley and floral
design. Brown and orange
on yellow speckled
ground. Cotton twill.

Variation in blue and
orange on yellow
speckled ground.

Variation of the batik-look floral print Navy blue, yellow, and terra cotta on beige.

Batik-look floral print. Forest green, yellow, and red-brown on beige. Combed cotton.

Variation of the batik-look floral print. Cranberry red, yellow, and cadet blue on beige.

Floral print in the batik style. Navy blue and terra cotta on cream. Cotton/rayon blend.

Variation of the floral print in the batik style. Orange and green on cream.

Variation of the floral print in the batik style. Orange and midnight blue on cream.

Flowers and leaves in a batik-look print. Multicolors on cream. Cotton/rayon blend.

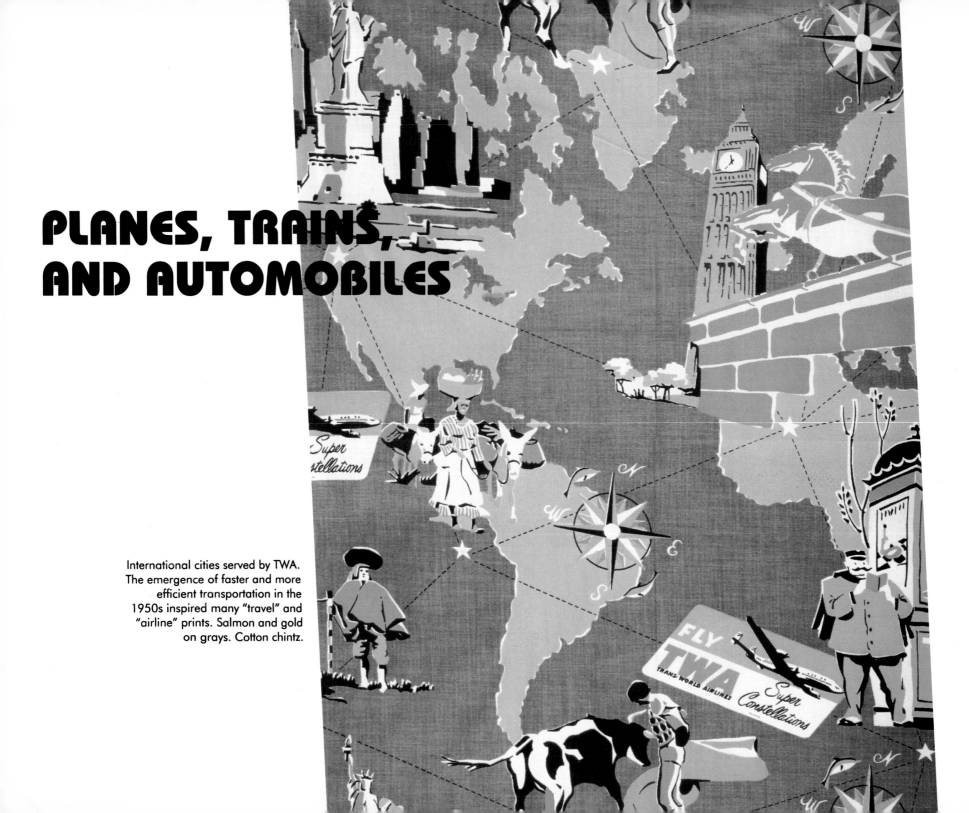

PLANES, TRAINS, AND AUTOMOBILES

International cities served by TWA. The emergence of faster and more efficient transportation in the 1950s inspired many "travel" and "airline" prints. Salmon and gold on grays. Cotton chintz.

Another view of the fabric design.

The entire swatch of the design.

Airline luggage labels and decals. Red, white, and blue on black. Cotton chintz.

Border print formed by trains and various railroad
images. Interestingly, the loop borders are formed by
the smoke. Multicolors on white ground. Polished cotton.

Cartoon-like
images of trains in
a one-directional,
horizontal stripe
pattern. Brown,
green, orange,
and yellow on
white. Open-
weave rayon/
linen blend.

Variation in
blues, red,
and yellow
on white.

Antique autos and "futuristic" license plates. Although this fabric was designed in the 1950s, the license plates read 1970. Blue, red, and green on off-white. Cotton/linen blend.

Different types of coaches set in a non-directional, boxed pattern. Pink, blue, taupe, and black on white. Polished cotton.

Early century automobiles. Green, orange,
and white on brick red. Cotton chintz.

Sports cars of the
1950s. Red and
blue on black.
Cotton chintz.

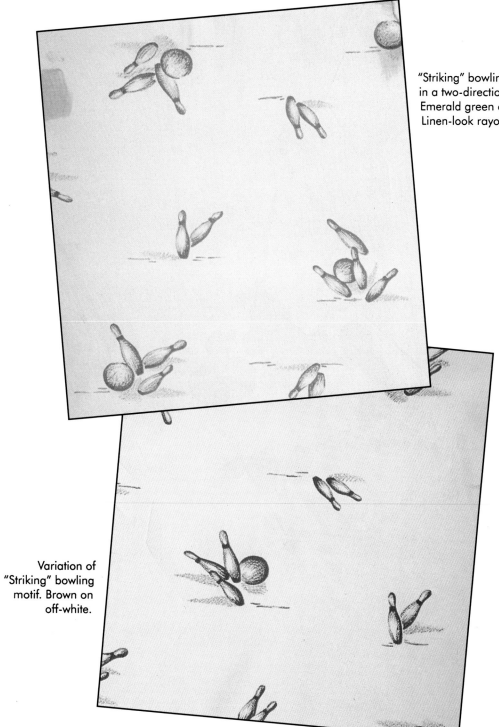

"Striking" bowling motif in a two-directional print. Emerald green on white. Linen-look rayon.

Variation of "Striking" bowling motif. Brown on off-white.

SPORTS AND RECREATION

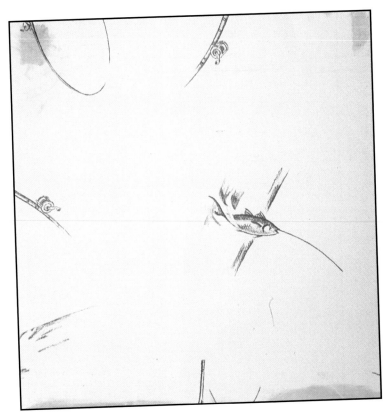

Fishing theme on a spaced, non-directional print Cadet blue on white. Rayon.

Fisherman and various fishing motifs in a two-directional print, cleverly framed by fishing poles and lines. Red, blue, and yellow on cream. Cotton/rayon blend.

Variation in blue and brown on yellow.

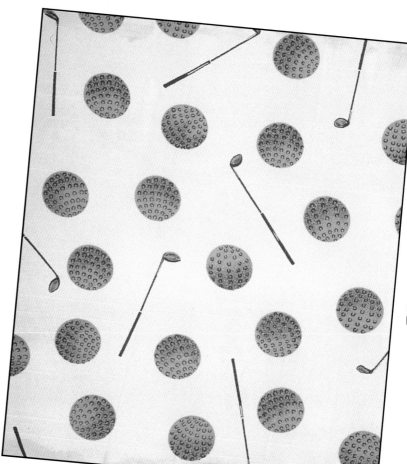

This dotted print features golf balls and clubs. Orange and brown on white. Linen-look rayon.

Variation in red, green, and yellow on light blue.

Three color variations of the golf theme print. Shown on slate blue and gray grounds, and bright red.

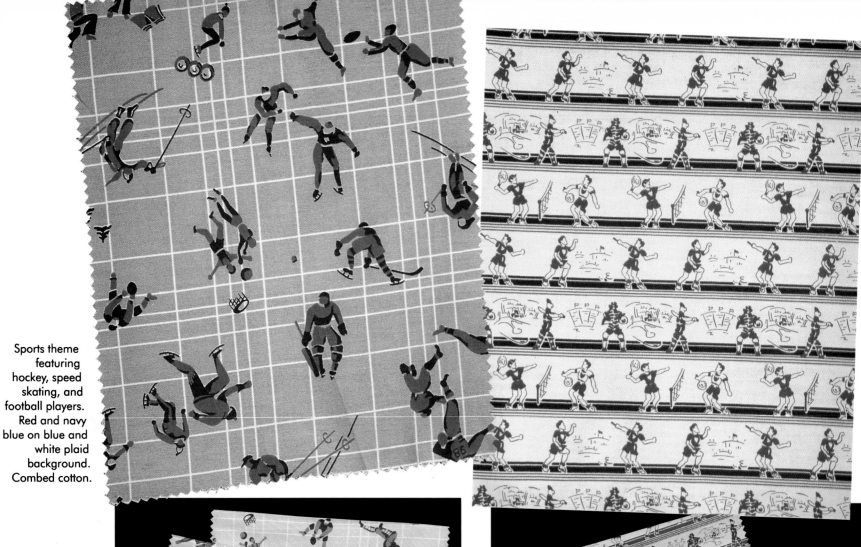

Sports theme featuring hockey, speed skating, and football players. Red and navy blue on blue and white plaid background. Combed cotton.

One-directional, horizontal stripes with sports theme. Maroon and blue on off-white. Cotton/rayon blend.

Variations of the fabric on yellow and taupe grounds.

Two variations shown in maroon and blue on light blue, and red and brown on yellow.

Close-up of sports-theme print. What
are the figures in the middle row doing?

Children outside a fence-in ballpark are depicted in this horizontal border design. Brown and blue on yellow. Cotton/rayon blend.

Two variations on light blue and off-white backgrounds.

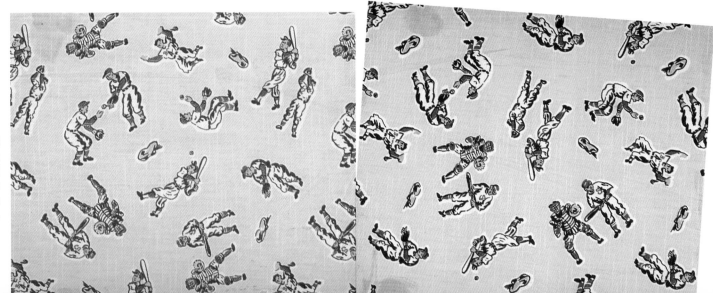

Baseball players in a non-directional print. Green and orange on yellow. Linen.

Variation in red and dark blue on sky blue.

Large images of baseballs create a background for players in the midst of a game. Red, yellow, and green on sky blue ground. Linen-look rayon.

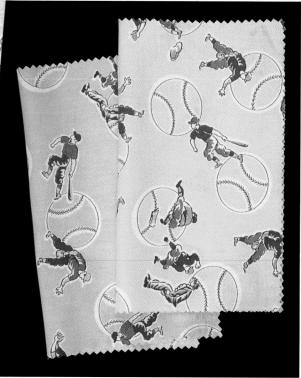

Two variations of the baseball print on yellow and beige grounds.

Alpine skiers in an embroidery-look one-directional, horizontal stripe pattern. Red, white, and blue. Linen.

Olympic rings and competitors in various poses. Red, yellow, and slate blue on light blue ground. Polished cotton.

Variation of the Olympic-theme print. Green, red, and brown on beige ground.

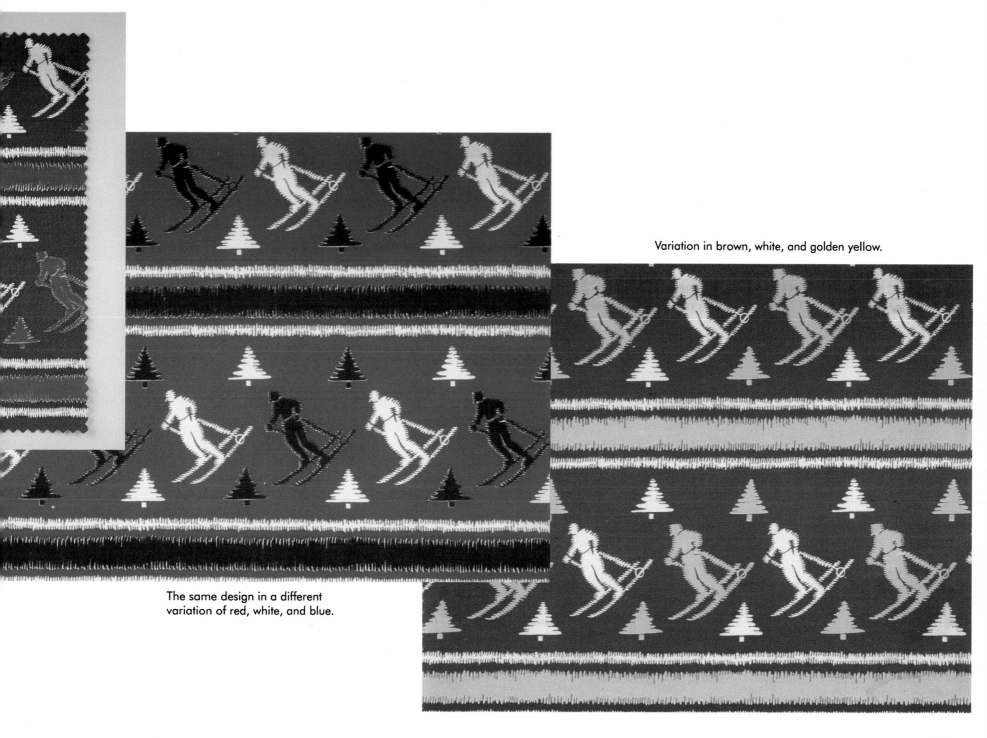

Variation in brown, white, and golden yellow.

The same design in a different
variation of red, white, and blue.

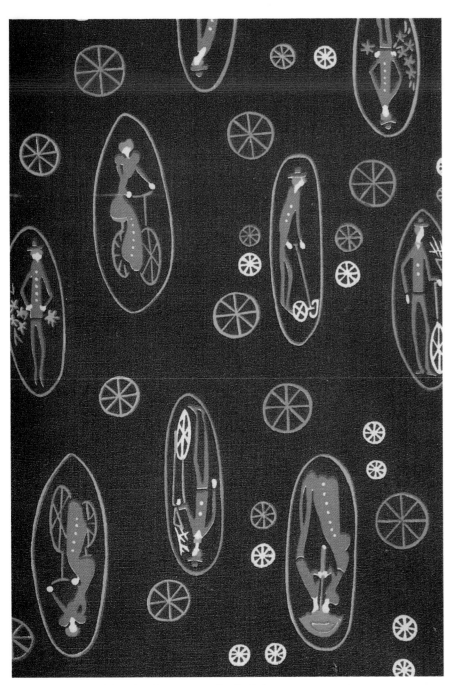

Victorian images on wheels. Salmon, green, and white on medium gray. Cotton/rayon blend.

Opposite:
Horse racing scenes at the tracks, in a one-directional pattern. Black, pink, and gold on brown. Polished cotton.

Right:
Variation in brown, black, and green on white.

Below:
Variation in blue, brown, black, and red on white.

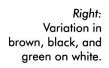

Variation in brown and black on blue.

CIRCUS AND CHILDREN'S THEMES

Amusement park theme, in a one-directional, horizontal stripe pattern. Blues, greens, and orange on yellow. Open weave linen/rayon blend.

Circus train with clowns and animals. One-directional print in red, yellow, and blues. Cotton/rayon blend.

The same design in a brighter yellow color.

Circus theme images in a non-directional scattered pattern. Primary colors on light blue ground. Cotton poplin.

Children's pattern with needlework effect, featuring a gingham checked stuffed animal. Red, blue, and green on white. Cotton chintz.

Alice in Wonderland characters in orange and green on peacock blue and white harlequin background. Polyester crepe.

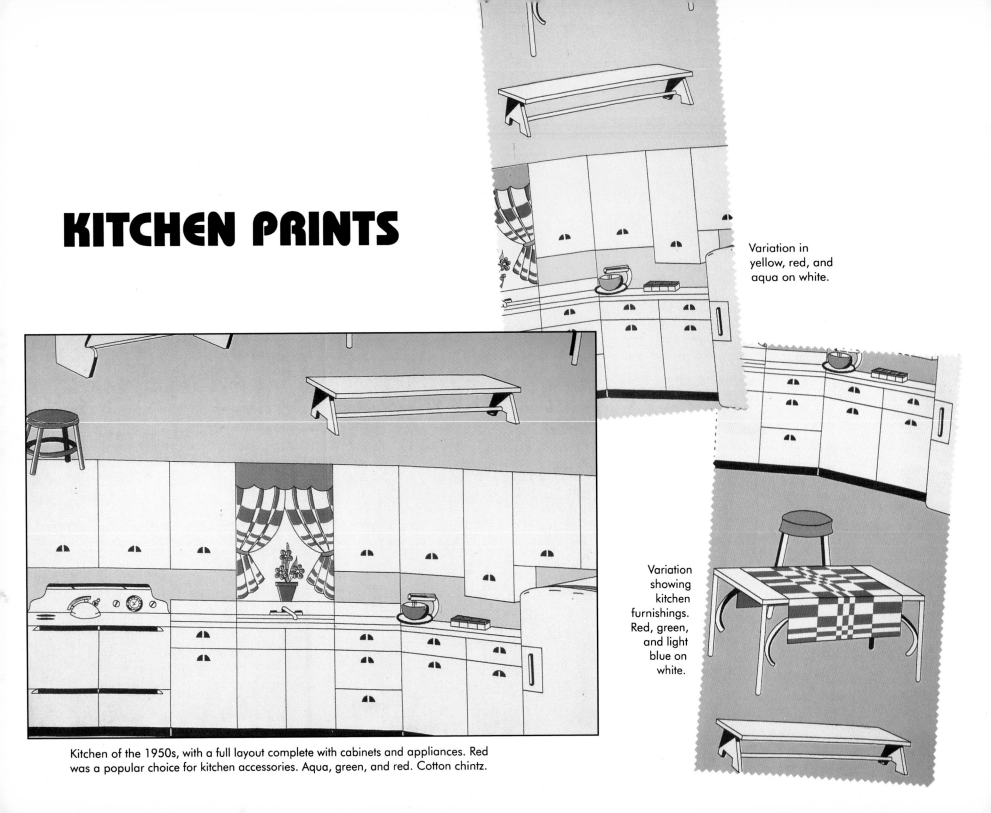

KITCHEN PRINTS

Variation in yellow, red, and aqua on white.

Variation showing kitchen furnishings. Red, green, and light blue on white.

Kitchen of the 1950s, with a full layout complete with cabinets and appliances. Red was a popular choice for kitchen accessories. Aqua, green, and red. Cotton chintz.

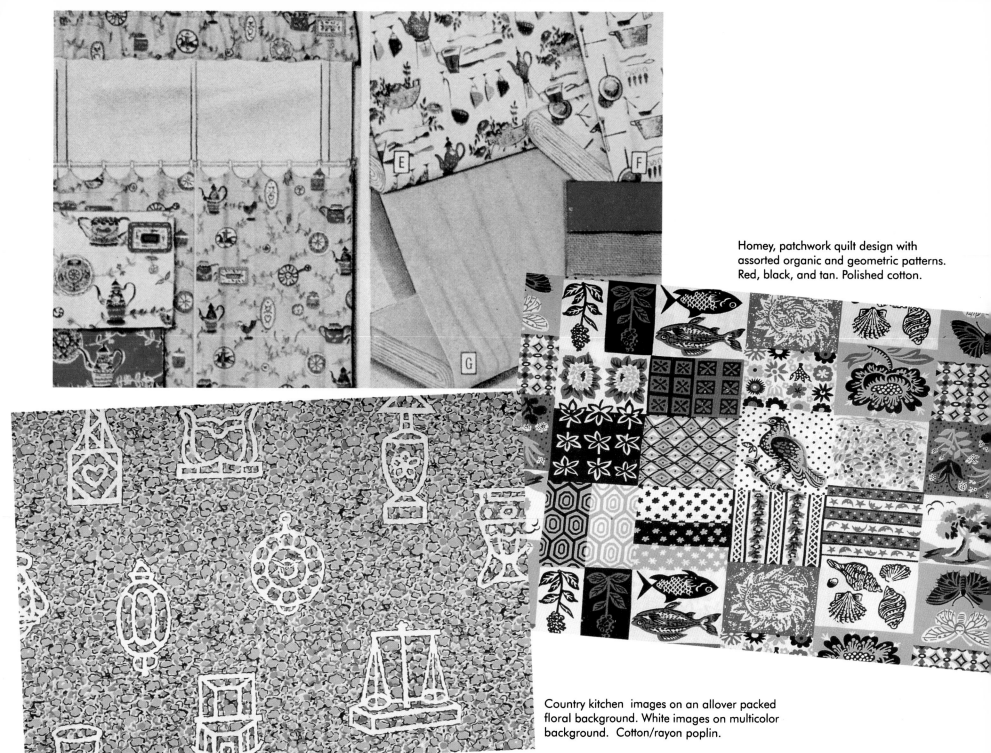

Homey, patchwork quilt design with assorted organic and geometric patterns. Red, black, and tan. Polished cotton.

Country kitchen images on an allover packed floral background. White images on multicolor background. Cotton/rayon poplin.

99

Fruit patterns on polka
dot background set in a
box layout. Pink and
red on black and white.
Cotton/rayon blend.

Juicy cherries tossed
in a non-directional
pattern. Red and
green on white.
Cotton chintz.

Pennsylvania Dutch-inspired images
encircled by colorful floral wreaths.
Multicolors on white. Cotton chintz.

100

Scattered, non-directional pattern with fruit, animal, and insect images. Brown ground. Cotton/rayon poplin.

Two color variations on gray and black ground. The contrasts in the black background design is most striking.

NOVELTY GEOMETRICS

Variations in greens and yellow.

Random geometric pattern in an abstract design in a classic late '50s style. Red and blues on white. Open weave linen/rayon blend.

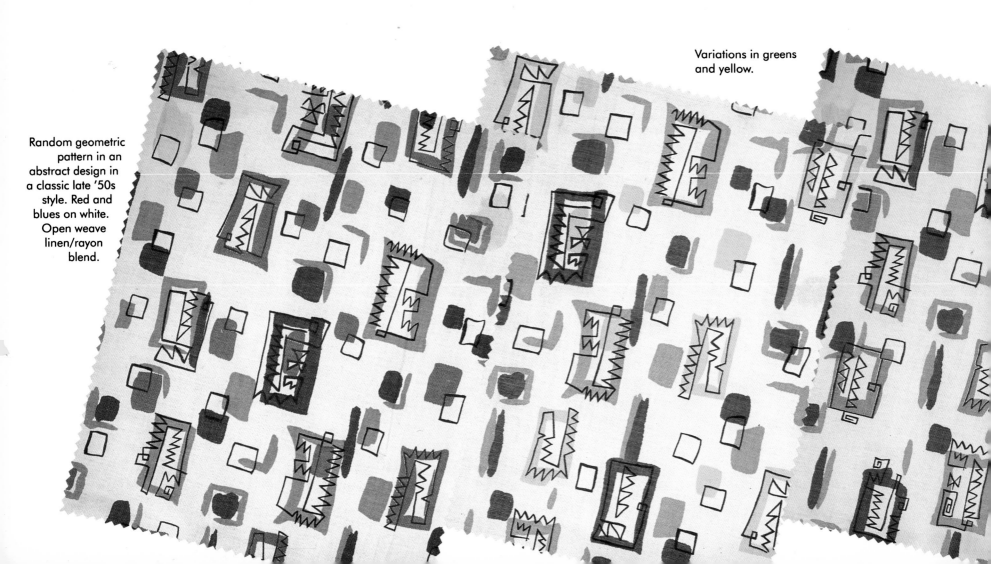

Waffle-look geometric shapes in a randomly tossed pattern. Red, gray, and white on royal blue. Brushed cotton.

Variations in browns and green.

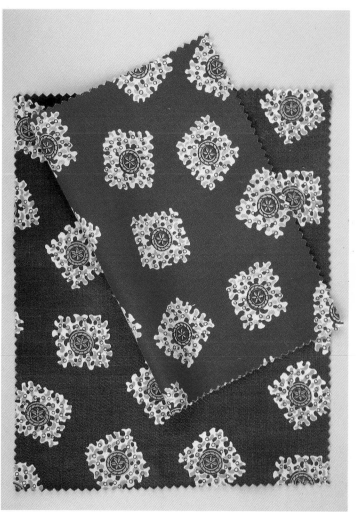

Variations on deep emerald green and cranberry red grounds.

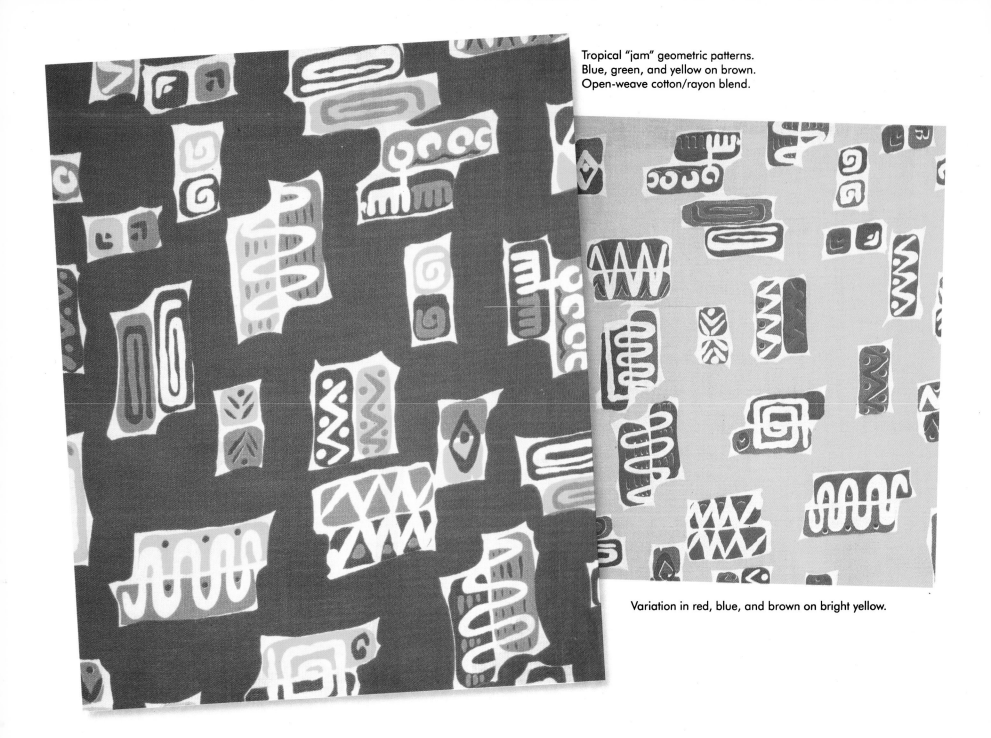

Tropical "jam" geometric patterns.
Blue, green, and yellow on brown.
Open-weave cotton/rayon blend.

Variation in red, blue, and brown on bright yellow.

104

Variation in
brown, red,
and yellow.

Diamond stripes with the look of a blue zig-zag pattern. It's not clear whether
this is a vertical or horizontal stripe. Red and gold on blue. Cotton chintz.

Variation in a lighter
color background.
Note how the color
change affects the
look of the overall
design. Green and
brown on pale yellow.

Two color variations of the same fabric.

Fretwork arranged in a random fashion. Black and gray on yellow. Cotton/rayon poplin.

Fretwork framed in different size boxes. Navy blue on white. Open weave linen/rayon blend.

Two variations on brown and green.

3 $15.74
24D2326

5 $13.74
24D2320

6 $12.74
24D2496

7 $9.74
24D2450

8 $7.67
24D2390

Interlocking geometric shapes in a honeycomb pattern. Blues on white. Rayon crepe.

Variations in green and brown.

Randomly placed squares, similar to the smaller foulard patterns found in men's ties. Red and lime green on deep forest green. Open weave cotton/linen blend.

Two variations on blue and brown.

Shields or family crests in a set medallion pattern with shadows.
Blue, brown, and black on white. Cotton/nylon crepe.

Closeup of pattern in green, orange, and black on white.

Geometric "eye-cons" in a scattered non-directional print. The images have a Native American-look but not enough to place it in that category. Green, white, and brown on bright yellow. Cotton/rayon blend.

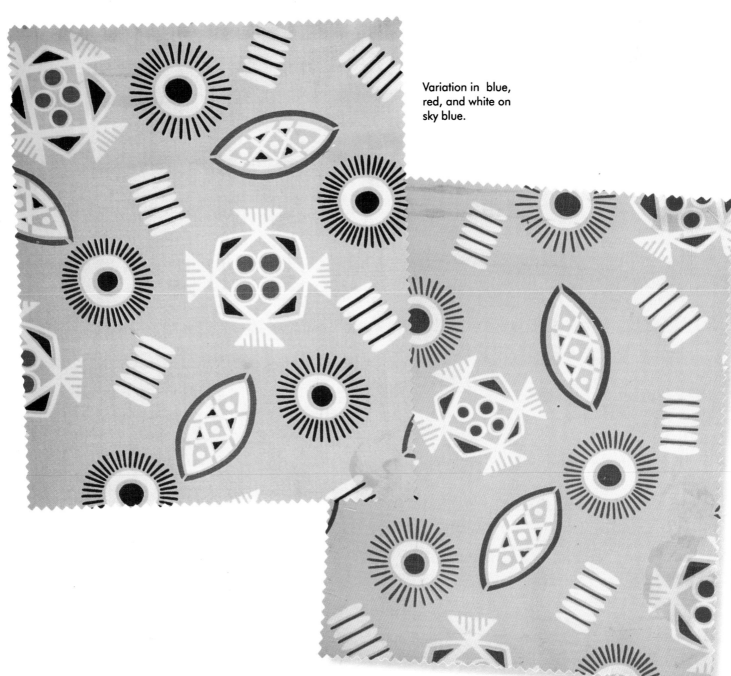

Variation in blue,
red, and white on
sky blue.

Variation in
dark green,
red, and white
on beige-pink.

111

Letters of the alphabet on starburst design. Orange, black, and brown on blue and white. Polyester crepe.

Three color variations on black, gray, and brown.